Retirement
Common Problems, Uncommon Solutions

MW01073334

Preface

When it comes to retirement, there are a lot of opinions out there about how you should handle your money. What you're about to read is **my** opinion. We all develop our opinions based on our personal experiences. The less personal experience one has with a particular subject the **less** we value their opinion. The more personal experience one has the **more** we value their opinion.

I have been coaching pre-retirees and retirees for over 20 years and I wont say that I've seen it all, but I have seen a lot! It's this experience that informs my opinions about the best strategies for my clients.

The problems and solutions I present are **not meant to be "all encompassing"** but I have found that most retirees do have concerns with one or more of them.

I consider myself a retirement coach not a financial planner. My experience coaching football for many years helps my clients define and achieve a plan for all phases of their retirement.

It's important to always remember that **financial planning and retirement planning are NOT the same thing.** What you're about to read will show you exactly what I mean!

This pyramid shows the process that we use with our clients and you are about to read the secrets and strategies that make this work!

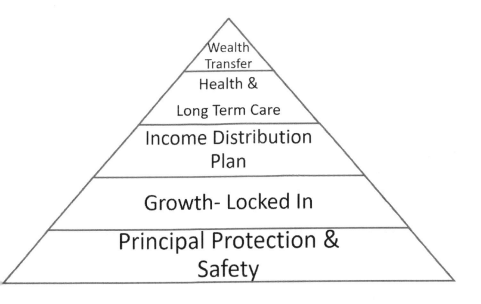

Chapter 1- Long Term Care Expenses

No one, and I mean **no one**, wants to think about health care and long-term healthcare costs as they're getting older. It's a morbid subject and can cause great distress and anxiety in most people and with good reason.

A lot of us may have horror stories of a family member or people that we love who are suffering in their older ages. We think about our own health failing and we often worry about the burden that could put on our loved ones.

That is a natural response towards the ones you love. Never apologize for that feeling.

My own grandmother spent over **ten years** residing in assisted living facilities, nursing homes and hospice. Needless to say, those experiences left her penniless and cost our family money that we never had planned to spend on her healthcare expenses.

All of us family members loved my grandmother with all our hearts so we never regretted all we did for her. But, it took a financial **toll** on us, yes.

Statistics show that the majority of money that you pay for your health care will be spent in the last part of your life.

That makes sense, of course. To be more specific, the last six months of your life will be your greatest financial hit!

The reality is this:

A lifetime of hard work and saving can vanish in the blink of an eye because of long-term health care expenses. Everything you sacrificed and struggled with as you finally reached the top of the financial mountain...

Gone.

I'm not trying to scare you here. But, reality is a great motivator and **NOW** is the time for you to be proactive and make certain this is not **your** financial destiny.

If you are in your 60s or 70s, it is never too late to plan for these expenses and have tremendous peace of mind knowing that neither you, nor your family, will be burdened with the stress of outliving your income and cash flow as you get older.

Statistics show that 70% of those over age 65 will need some form of long-term care.

Sadly, for most people their plan is extremely limited; forcing them to choose between either **self-pay or state pay.**

What am I talking about here?

Self-pay means exactly what it sounds like. You are paying for your health care expenses; specifically long-term health care expenses.

If you have not purchased a long-term care insurance policy in your 50s the likelihood of you purchasing one in your 60s and 70s goes with each passing year.

The longer you wait to buy this insurance; the more expensive and difficult it will be to qualify for the medical benefits you need to survive.

Self-pay does not always mean you are paying for it. But, **someone** will be. It could be your children or grandchildren that are paying the facilities or for home care.

But, either way this falls into the category of self-pay.

Then, there is the **alternative.**

State pay is government-subsidized for lower income and asset levels and **Medicaid** is your only option here as a resident of the United States. It is a welfare program that provides healthcare for the indigent.

If you've been to a Medicaid facility recently you wouldn't let your distant neighbors, much less your relatives go there. You certainly wouldn't want to put yourself in one for sure, trust me!

In order to qualify for Medicaid you must prove to the state that you are financially in need. This can be a humbling and humiliating process, especially for those who've worked very hard in their lives and in their careers to avoid being poor.

And ironically; they find themselves in a program that defines what they have spent their entire lives avoiding.

Embarrassing.

I think you'll agree neither of these options are a good plan.

But, sadly these are the main options left for most of us Americans.

The average cost for long-term care in 2018 is staggering. Here are the numbers:

Residing in an assisted living facility costs $40,000 or more a year. A nursing home is more expensive to the tune of $60,000 a year or more. A home health aide will cost you $22.00 an hour or more.

There is a healthcare crisis in America as we all know and my personal opinion is that the only way the free-market can fix this is if insurance companies, healthcare providers, doctors and anyone engaged in providing healthcare AND the insurance industry **voluntarily** agree to be less profitable!

Do you really think that is going to happen?

I don't either.

So we are left with a mixed bag of frustration when it comes to the most important area of our lives in old age: **Health care.**

Some of the costs will be provided to us through welfare and entitlements. Some of them will be provided through our own hard-earned money or spent on expensive insurance claims with high deductibles.

But, the harsh reality is that I don't see this changing, in fact I see our health care costs going even **higher.**

So, what's the solution?

The **traditional** way to take care of this problem and have peace of mind is to **purchase long-term care insurance.**

This would be the advice your financial advisor, insurance broker or even a close friend or family member would give you when it comes to having a financial plan and peace of mind in your retirement.

Unfortunately long term care insurance is a **"dog"** for insurance companies.

Here's what I mean by that.

Long Term Care insurance is **not** a profitable product for insurance companies to offer the average consumer. And, if you know anything about insurance companies if it isn't profitable, it isn't likely.

Insurance, after all, is **pooling** risk. When you have policyholders making claims (some of them very big claims) on their long-term care insurance policies this becomes extremely costly for insurance companies.

When the risk pool becomes expensive for an insurance company what do they do?

Raise the price of that insurance for everyone in the risk pool.

As a result, many long-term care insurance providers have actually pulled out of that market because they could not afford to offer that insurance product to the general public and sustain a profit.

In fact, it's almost impossible to find a good long-term care insurance policy these days. And, if you do find one, it may be extremely difficult to qualify for it medically.

No insurance company wants to pay a 10-year nursing home claim. So, they jack up the price and make them unaffordable.

You may still be able to buy one but you will pay outlandishly for it.

Outside of the fact that it's more difficult now than ever to find a good and inexpensive long-term care insurance policy, there is another more important reason not to buy one.

Let me explain.

Long-term care insurance is much like car insurance. **It's use-it-or-lose-it insurance!**

You probably paid for your car insurance every month of every year of your life since you were old enough to drive.

If you never have an accident and never made an accident claim your savings were probably **minimal** meaning that you paid almost as much as those who did not have your excellent driving record.

It is the same with your long-term care insurance. <u>You may be paying for insurance you won't even use;</u> like throwing money down the toilet.

Like going to Vegas...same thing!

To reinforce this concept: 70% of us over the age of 65 will need **some** form of long-term care. If you are in the 30% that doesn't need long-term care but purchased a long-term care insurance policy, you just **lined the pockets** of those insurance companies!

So, to summarize here:

#1. Long-term healthcare costs are something no one wants to think about and no one wants to spend money on while they're healthy. That is human nature.

#2. Most individual's plan for long-term care expenses is to pay for it out of their **own** pockets or become so indigent that the **state** will pay for it through Medicaid.

#3. Your current financial advisor, insurance broker, friends and even close family members will give you a single piece of advice when it comes to peace of mind in your retirement around long-term health care expenses.

Buy a Long-term care insurance policy!

#4. Long-term care insurance is very expensive, hard to qualify for medically, hard to find a good policy and if you don't make a claim, you just wasted your money!

Now on to the **solution.**

I call this: **Hybrid Long-Term Care.**

The technical name for this solution is a modified endowment contract or M. E. C.

Another name for this is current asset-based long-term care.

Here's how this works.

Most people in their 50s, 60s and 70s have some money lying around for a rainy day.

What does a rainy day mean when you're retired?

It could mean money to pay for unexpected expenses, vacations, major material purchases like homes and cars, helping out children or even friends and family that are in need.

In other words it is money that is not earmarked for one particular thing other than a "rainy day".

Remember now, no one thinks about spending this money to pay for their long-term health expenses. Maybe in the back of your mind the thought is there that this money **could** be spent on those things but you'd rather spend it improving your life or the lives of others around you.

The advice I am going to give you here is to take that rainy day money and **buy a hybrid long-term care policy.** This product will significantly leverage these funds from **day one!**

For example your $100,000 rainy day fund could immediately become a $200,000 benefit pool to use for long-term care expenses. I am not exaggerating here.

You are literally buying this leverage with your current good health. And, you don't have to be in nearly as good of health to qualify for hybrid long-term care as you do to qualify for a traditional long-term care insurance policy.

Remember what I said about traditional long-term care insurance. If you don't **need** care you don't get any benefit, just like car insurance.

With current asset-based hybrid long-term care, if you don't need care you don't PAY FOR IT. You don't lose a dime!

Your rainy day fund is never touched. It is completely intact.

If you do need care you have significant leverage the day you buy that policy.

In some cases (depending on your age and gender) you can more than double your rainy day fund to use to pay for your long-term care expenses.

And, here is another benefit.

With these types of insurance policies, your rainy day fund will **never** be taxed if it is used to pay for long-term care expenses. These policies will pay tax-free benefits out of the leveraged benefit pool for terminal illness, nursing home care, and chronic illness.

These are defined by being unable to perform two of six activities of daily living which are bathing, eating, toileting, dressing and ambulation.

These policies are also designed for those who may never need care. They are the fairest insurance policies you will ever buy, folks!

The growth potential of these policies is tremendous and there is never ever any downside risk. The benefit pool **grows** as you earn interest on the policy and there is never any limit on growth.

If you decide you don't want the policy anymore you get all of your rainy day fund back **plus** interest.

This creates peace of mind in you knowing you haven't flushed your money away on a policy that you'll never use.

Your current advisor, insurance broker, friends and family more than likely do not know about these types of policies. In fact there are only a handful of these available in the United States.

One more thing;

Let's say you decide you want to keep the policy for many years and you never make a claim on the leveraged pool of benefits for long-term care. Your beneficiaries will receive whatever the leveraged benefit pool has grown to on your death... completely **tax free!**

To recap, my recommendation is a hybrid long-term care insurance policy that is paid for with your rainy day money and leveraged immediately (sometimes as much as 100%) to pay for your long-term care expenses.

If you need to make a claim on the long-term care benefits you get them completely tax free.

If you don't need to make a claim on the long-term care benefits your rainy day fund remains intact plus interest. Interest is earned based on a portion of the growth of a major stock index with none of the risk ever.

You may choose to withdraw all of your funds plus interest at any time with **no** penalty.

Should you decide to keep the policy and you pass away while you own it, your beneficiaries get the entire benefit pool paid to them tax free.

Chapter 2 - Low Interest Rates and Inflation

One of my favorite sayings is, **"You've worked hard for your money, now make it work hard for you!"**

These words mean a lot to me because they define what motivates me as a retirement coach and drive my passion to help retirees in the sunset years of their very special lives.

Your money must work for you in retirement because you're not working for it any more. When your money isn't working for you I call this **lazy money!**

Wall Street and traditional retirement planning will tell you that the best way to keep pace with inflation is to buy low-cost mutual funds and other speculative investments and let them grow as long as you can.

Then, follow the 2, 3, 4 or 5% withdrawal rate rule.

For a lot of people this just isn't enough money to live on in retirement and taking this kind of risk to achieve that small withdrawal rate will not give you any peace of mind in retirement.

Traditional retirement planning will also tell you there are three levels of risk tolerance for investors: **conservative, moderate and aggressive.**

My personal opinion is the only acceptable level of risk for your retirement dollars is **zero or none.**

Let me make it a bit clearer; NO RISK is the only acceptable level!

America's cowboy, Will Rogers, once stated: I care more about the return **of** my money than the return **on** my money. I think he was specifically speaking to retirees here.

Warren Buffett's two rules of investing are:
#1: Don't lose money
#2: See Rule #1!

I'll cover more on investment risk later.

For now, let's assume that you've decided that taking any risk with your retirement money is not what you're going to do and are looking for the best place to keep your money safe and liquid and **GROWING!**

And like most people you have made the decision to place your precious retirement dollars in an account that is **growing at a very low rate of interest.**

After all, the less risk you take the less growth you get and the more risk you take the more growth you may get.

Whether it's a bank CD, money market account or any other fixed interest bearing savings account, this is not a position where your money will work for you.

This is absolutely, positively a lazy money position. You're not doing this because **you're** lazy, stupid, uninformed or ignorant.

You're probably doing it for **two** very good reasons.

One, you know it's safe and in most cases FDIC insured.

Two, you know you can get access to your money very easily if you need to.

Banks, bonds, and other fixed interest bearing accounts have been used for hundreds of years as a safe place for you to put your money. But again, you will not keep pace with inflation and you certainly won't meaningfully grow your money in these positions.

This is not only a lazy position but it is also a terrible position from a standpoint of taxes. Interest earned in these kinds of accounts is taxed as ordinary income; not as capital gains.

And, ordinary income as we all know is taxed **every** year whether you like it or not.

I want to pause and ask you **two important questions** that I'll answer later in this book:

Why is it that your money at risk is taxed at a lower rate than your money in a safe position?

Why is it that your job wages and the money you earn while you're working is taxed at a much higher rate than your investments?

The answer to this may shock you because you will clearly see there is a big difference between savings and investments.

What I'm talking about here is savings, money that you can access easily and that isn't at risk.

I've painted a picture of a situation that many, many retirees are in. You've decided you no longer want to risk your money in investments and you want to place it in a safe position.

It cannot make any significant money for you. Your money is not working for you.

I don't want you to get the impression that banks or safe positions are a terrible idea. They are a logical, safe and conservative idea but not a great idea.

You can do so much **better.**

It's like buying a Ferrari and once a month driving it around the block at 20 mph and parking back in your garage. It's safe but it is not doing what you had intended it for when you paid all that money in purchasing it!

To be honest with you, I take issue with the way banks handle people's money. Banks are experts at creating **arbitrage.**

Arbitrage is the difference in the interest rate on money that is **given** to the bank vs. money that is **borrowed** from the bank. And, if you've ever taken a loan from a bank or put your money in a bank you'll know there is a very big **difference.**

Banks lend your money out at **XX.X%** and pay you **.XX%.** This is how it has always worked and this is the sacrifice that today's retirees make for safety and liquidity.

Yes banks charge a ton of interest to borrowers! Consider when you take out a loan from a bank or other lending institution; in many cases they use whats called an "amortization schedule". The "interest rate" is not what it seems. It's much higher!

Has your money ever **earned** interest based on an "amortization schedule"?

Didn't think so.

These institutions are not your financial friends. They exist to make money not to make you rich. They're banks!

A word on inflation here.

My father always used this analogy when talking about inflation. He would say, "A quality baseball glove costs the same now as it did in 1955: $30.00. But, the cost of a gallon of gas is 20 times **more** expensive!"

His point was, **inflation doesn't affect every area of our lives but it does where it counts.**

With technology, cell phones, televisions etc. we see deflation and manufactures can produce these products for less and less as the years go by. However, housing and transportation are another story.

What are the 2 biggest expenses everyone (not just retirees) have?

Housing and transportation!

As a retiree, **where do you want to spend your money** and are you going to spend it on things that are heavily affected by inflation or not as affected?

Where your money is positioned will **determine** what you will be able to buy and the lifestyle you will live in retirement. I am about to provide you with is a solution that I believe is the best of three worlds.

Safety, liquidity and growth.

But before that let's recap: Traditionally you only have two choices when it comes to where you'll position your retirement dollars.

Investments; which have risk and, **safety** which has **no** risk but very little growth or protection against inflation.

Safety positions are lazy positions and your money is not working for you there!

Fixed interest is taxed as ordinary income every year like it or not and you don't get the benefit of the lower capital gains tax rate. Banks are professionally skilled at paying as little interest possible to the lender and charging as high of interest as possible to the borrower.

Their practice does not allow your money to work for you.

Inflation affects everyone in different ways and you need to analyze where you will spend your money in retirement to see how inflation will affect you.

The solution?

Indexed insurance contracts. These can come in the form of a MEC as I described in Chapter 1 or as an Indexed annuity.

I'd like to address a couple of major concerns people have when it comes to **annuities**.

You may have heard horror stories of people investing in annuities and not getting their money back. This situation can still occur and has occurred. It happens when you purchase a life-only annuity strategy.

Life-only income payments will continue for exactly that long;

Life Only!

If you purchase an annuity with $100,000 and your annual payment is $10,000 for your life it sounds good; but if you pass away in three years after purchasing that annuity you only receive $30,000!

Who gets the remaining $70,000?

The insurance company

Yes, they are very similar to banks in monitoring your money in their favor.

Needless to say, this is a **BAD** strategy and should not be employed!

Unless of course you are psychic and are sure you will live to be 100 years old!

Also, annuities contain surrender charges. You need to be aware that a full withdrawal of your money **prior** to the contract term expiring could result in a penalty paid by **you.**

It's important to meet with an independent financial representative who can show you numerous different products to ensure you that you're buying the annuity that best **fits** your needs.

Another product I believe you should avoid is a variable annuity.

A variable annuity is just a mutual fund WITH extra fees, loads and surrender charges.

With these products you get all of the risks AND all of the costs!

For these reasons, annuities have been maligned by some experts in traditional financial planning. I believe that life-only annuity strategies, high surrender charge annuity products and variable annuities should **not** be recommended to retirees.

What I do believe is that you should purchase an **indexed insurance contract.**

What does that mean?

It is the ability to earn annual credited interest based on the <u>majority of growth in a major stock index,</u> without being directly invested in that index.

These products were created in 1996 by some very smart people. Insurance actuaries and financial specialists developed a strategy that used investment grade bonds and other fixed interest instruments within the annuity contract, along with the purchasing **stock options** in a major stock index.

What they created was a product that would allow for the majority of stock index growth to be credited to the annuity contract every year with **no risk** to the contract holder.

The insurance company bears all of the investment risk; not the consumer.

So, the most important thing to know about these contracts is this:

If the stock market is doing well, you will be doing well. Much better than you could ever do in any other type of fixed interest bearing account! If the stock market is doing poorly the only risk you take is to the amount of interest you'll earn and the worst you can do is 0%.

Please understand that **a fixed indexed annuity is not an investment;** it is an insurance contract and savings vehicle with lifetime income options.

However, in most other fixed savings vehicles when you have non-qualified money, interest earned is taxed annully, with annuities and indexed insurance contracts, interest is **tax deferred** until you withdraw it!

A question I am often asked is: "If the interest in my annuity is credited based on the growth of a major stock index, which index do the insurance companies use and which one is the best?"

It is far and away the **S&P 500**.

The S&P 500 is 500 stocks in every major sector of the American economy.

Check out this quote,

"Over the last 15 years, 92.2% of large Cap funds lagged a simple S&P 500 index fund. The percentages of mid-cap and small-Cap funds lagging their benchmarks were even higher: 95.4% and 93.2%, respectively" – Market Watch, May 13th 2017.

In other words, most mutual funds cannot beat the S&P 500. They never have and they never will!

So to summarize: What you get with an **indexed insurance contract** is the ability to earn credited interest that can perform right along with the stock market when it's doing well and only show a 0% rate of return when it isn't.

There are never any losses!

With these products you can make your money work for you!

And, isn't that the point?

Chapter 3- Taxable Inheritance and Estate

Taxes, much like the **end of life** healthcare expenses, are also something nobody really wants to think about.

No matter which side of the political spectrum you lean, I think we can all agree we'd like to pay less taxes; especially in the **latter** years of our lives.

Because you don't have predictable and consistent income coming in as you prepare to retire; different considerations need to be made with regard to how you're going to spend and save your money.

Your hard-earned money needs to be preserved so you can enjoy retirement and have tremendous peace of mind!

We need to begin with **taxes.**

I want to address what I think are the biggest flaws in our tax system that pertain to retirees, particularly a very **specific** kind of tax. The one that your loved ones will have to pay after you're gone.

Traditional retirement planning will tell you that the way to take care of this tax is with **life insurance.**

There are two main types of life insurance: **Permanent** and **term.** Either one is a big winner for insurance companies. The main reason is that **half** of the people who buy either of these **never** make a death claim.

Yes, you read this amazing fact correctly!

Half the people who own **term** insurance either stop paying premiums and lapse the policy or they outlive the insurance term. And, people who buy **permanent** insurance either stop paying premiums or cash the policy out entirely.

In either case, this puts big profits in the pockets of insurance companies and the agents who sell them.

So, let's talk about how traditional retirement planning that involves savings products and investments are **taxed** on your passing.

Your qualified accounts meaning IRAs and 401 K's are taxed as **ordinary** income. Here's what that means.

When your beneficiaries receive these accounts on your passing, the entire amount is taxed at their **current ordinary income tax rate.**

Here is a fact you need to be aware of here:

Studies show that most beneficiaries spend their inheritance very <u>quickly</u> once they receive it!

One way to minimize this is by structuring a **stretch** account or a stretch IRA. They allow the custodian or overseer of your qualified account to pay the monies to your beneficiaries **over time based on their life expectancy.**

This can be a good strategy to allow the account to continue to grow and minimize taxes.

However there's no avoiding taxation on a **qualified** account. Even if it is done slowly, taxes must always be paid.

But, if you have a qualified account that it is earmarked for inheritance some experts are recommending a strategy where you cash the IRA or 401(k) out **completely** and pay all the taxes while you're alive and then purchase a life insurance policy in its stead.

I recommend this strategy under the **right** circumstances but there is a very <u>specific</u> type of life insurance policy that should be used here. More on that later.

If you have savings accounts like the ones discussed in the previous chapter those accounts are also taxed upon your death. But, if they are **non-qualified** accounts only the interest is taxed not the principal unless your estate exceeds the current exemption amount for estate taxes.

A significant savings to you!

Your investments, meaning stocks, bonds and mutual funds will also become taxable to your beneficiaries **if** they sell off your investment positions.

However they are taxed at the **current capital gains tax rate** not the ordinary income tax rate.

Here's the **dilemma** for people in their late 50's, 60's and 70's when it comes to purchasing life insurance.

It's hard to qualify for medically.

You're not a spring chicken anymore.

In fact, most insurers will not issue term insurance to people **over age 60**. They want young healthy people purchasing term insurance who they know will probably never make a death claim.

Like Vegas casinos, these are house rules designed to make profits here.

For younger people it's really more like **accidental** death insurance not insurance designed to provide a death benefit for health-related issues.

If you own annuities that are earmarked for inheritance and they're non-qualified accounts, all of the interest earned in those accounts will become **taxable** as ordinary income to your beneficiaries.

Talk this over with your financial consultant so you can clearly see how insurance companies operate here.

Any monies you have when you pass away that are not in a life insurance policy will be **taxable** to your beneficiaries! So, you are trapped there, too.

Let's summarize and then move on to my solution.

1. When younger folks buy life insurance it's a big moneymaker for insurance companies because at least half of them never make a death claim.

2. The older you are the harder it gets to purchase a good life insurance policy that fits your needs.

3. Your beneficiaries will not be able to avoid taxation on any of the money they inherit that is in traditional retirement savings products or investments.

Now, let me remedy some of these drawbacks for you.

My solution here is a **modified endowment contract** (M.E.C.).

Let me use an example to **illustrate** how this could work.

Let's say you're 65 years-old and you have $100,000 that you'd like to be able to pass along to your beneficiaries and do it in the most **tax efficient way** possible. You can purchase a M.E.C. that immediately doubles your $100,000 to $200,000 for your beneficiaries.

(Disclaimer: this is the typical amount of leverage that someone aged 65 years old could expect with these products but the exact amount will **vary** by your age, gender and whether you're a tobacco user)

So, you now have at least $200,000 in a death benefit that will be payable to your beneficiaries completely **tax free** upon your passing.

This $200,000 may also be used to pay for your long-term health care expenses and those benefits are also paid **tax free**!

This "pool of benefits" can never go backwards!

It grows at an interest rate based on index credits as I discussed in the previous chapter.

Remember, for those individuals over the age of 60, health problems and the time consuming and invasive process of underwriting and qualifying for life insurance are the biggest **barriers** to obtaining the amount of coverage that your spouse and children need.

This particular type of life insurance policy has an underwriting process that is referred to as a, **"simplified issue."**

This means you do **not** have to take a medical exam, provide a blood or urine sample or submit all of your medical records.

Instead, these products typically have 10 health questions that you'll have to answer and then the insurance company looks at the medical information based on your answers to make a **determination** on insuring you.

You don't have to be in what I call, **"astronaut"** health to be able to qualify for these policies. They are specifically designed for people over the age of 55.

If you've had recent major surgeries, hospitalizations, cancer or severe diabetes you will **not** be able to qualify; but most folks in "good to average" health will qualify here.

But here's what makes these policies so much different than the **term** and **permanent** life insurance policies previously mentioned.

If you decide at some point in the future after purchasing a M.E.C. contract that you don't want it anymore **you can completely cash it out and not lose a dime of the principal amount that you purchased it with!**

You'll receive **all** your money back plus interest.

More than likely, you will earn much better interest on your money in one of these products than you would in a traditional fixed interest-bearing savings vehicle.

How can this be?

Here is the short answer: These products are actuarially priced for **older** people and the insurance carriers know they can't provide as much death benefit leverage for someone who is 60 years old as they can for someone who is 30 years old.

But I'd say doubling (or better) the amount of money that you already have earmarked for your beneficiaries is a pretty good deal; especially considering that they'll inherit it totally **tax free**.

There are only a handful of these products available and most likely your current financial advisor or insurance broker will not have knowledge of these types of products.

These products are a dog for insurance companies because you're <u>not giving them as much money</u> as you would with **term** insurance or other kinds of **permanent** life insurance products.

M.E.C'S are always considered **"paid up"** insurance. In other words, you make one premium payment in the beginning and you never have to put in any more money in after that.

Plus, this kind of policy will **never** lapse!

One last caveat: There's no way to purchase life insurance with **qualified** funds. However, if the monies you have earmarked for inheritance are qualified funds, you can still purchase a M.E.C. with one premium payment and slowly pay the taxes on the qualified account over five or ten years.

And, you don't have to write a check to the IRS; the insurance company does that **for** you.

If this information has you intrigued I highly recommend doing some research to find **a simplified issue, indexed modified endowment contract** that is best for you.

Just be aware these policies are very rare and they're not that easy to find. But, when you do, **they are GOLD!**

Chapter 4 - Market Risk

The first three chapters of this book were focused on two issues that people don't want to think about and don't really want to plan for:

Death and **old age healthcare expenses**.

I can't control the first problem but I can help you successfully manage the second one.

The biggest question everyone nearing retirement has is:

"How much income will I have and what will my monthly expenses be?"

Obviously, the time for you to confront this question is **now;** not later. Chances are if you are on the verge of retirement you are only now beginning to face this question.

And, why is THAT?

Because when you were making money you always had a financial option to fall back on.

Guess what?

For most of you that is no longer the case.

You are not going to be working anymore and you will lose the peace of mind that a consistent paycheck provides.

We'd like to maintain the same lifestyle we had when when we were working; or even a much better lifestyle!

When clients come into my office they always have one of these two major concerns:

How much risk am I taking with my retirement savings and how much income can my portfolio generate for me in retirement.

The two are very closely related and very important.

In this chapter I'm going to be focusing on **risk**. As I said in a previous chapter I believe the only acceptable risk tolerance level is **zero or none.**

Traditional financial planning and Wall Street meets with clients to ask them, **"What is your risk tolerance level?"**

This is part of their planning process and then they also look at **time horizon.** The longer the time horizon, the riskier investments advisors and brokers will suggest for you. The shorter the time horizon, the less risky.

Some may use the "Rule of 100". Here, you take 100 and subtract your current age and that number is the percentage of assets that should be placed in a "risk" position.

This has been a tried and true financial planning process because as any good advisor knows, over the long run, the stock market does well.

Studies show in the history of the stock market as a whole, **the average rate of return on an annual basis is around 10%.** And the bull market run we've had in the last 10 years should add to that average.

This is exactly why stocks, bonds, mutual funds, ETF's and other types of equity and debt-based investments have been the most popular way for people to make their money work for them.

My opinion is however, that these types of investment recommendations are **not a good fit** for those 60 and older.

Let me explain why.

As you are getting older you obviously have a shorter time horizon for your investments. You no longer have the 20, 30 or 40 years that you did when you were working to ride out the ups and downs of the stock market.

Very important point here: **you don't have to risk your principle to receive reasonable, or even very good rates of return!** More on that soon.

The stock market is for speculators, risk takers and market makers and when you're young you can **afford** to be a speculator and risk taker. We've seen two major market corrections in last 20 years and if you got scared and sold off your positions, you may have realized some tremendous losses within your portfolio.

But, if you had the time and means to ride out those corrections you probably did pretty well; maybe very well.

When you're working, you're saving and accumulating and not using your savings to live off of; you have your wages to do that. So whatever is happening with your money you can look the other way and just hope everything works out.

Some advisors even tell investors: "Quit looking at your account statements." This is fine advice if you don't currently need that money to live on.

If you <u>do</u> need that money to live on, you should be MUCH more concerned with the current value of your accounts, right?

Your nest egg **must last you all the way through your retirement** and I simply don't feel it is anything that should be put at any risk whatsoever. Make sense?

When clients work with me, I don't waste time asking what their risk tolerance is; I believe in a zero or no risk tolerance for clients over the age of 60.

I mentioned the 10% average rate of return but when it comes to these types of investments, averages can be deceiving.

If you look at the most successful mutual funds of all time, (Magellen, Vanguard) these funds have shown very nice double digit annual rates of return in their long and storied histories.

But many studies have been done to see if those who owned these funds **actually** earned these average rates of return on their money... and guess what?

They did not!

The averages are only if you purchased the fund when it started and sold it today (or when it was no longer available). People who buy in early or late have vastly different rates of return.

And, an "average annual rate of return" is a ridiculous concept when it comes to mutual funds and other speculative investments because **NONE** of these "returns" are ever truly realized unless you sell the investment!

You get what you get at the time you sell it. It's that simple.

And, this point is exactly why risk, I believe, should not be in your portfolio **once you reach 60 years of age.**

No one has ever been able to play the market and time it perfectly. Except maybe Warren Buffet. There will always be **winners and losers.**

I'm going to present a solution for you that allows your money to be credited with actual interest, not capital gains or paper gains but actual, annual credited interest based on the growth of a major stock index. No losses, only WINS!

If you've already read the first two chapters, you know what index I'm talking about.

Before I present you with the solution, I had mentioned earlier I wanted to talk about the major difference between the capital gains tax rate and the ordinary income tax rate.

Your investments are taxed at a much lower rate than your wages and earnings from your working career. This has never made any sense to me and maybe you haven't ever thought about it but it seems rather unfair that **your blood sweat and tears is taxed at a higher rate than your investments are.**

This is my theory on why the tax rate is so different between these two.

If you want to save for retirement, you were told by Wall Street, the **only** way to do it is was stocks, bonds, mutual funds, equities and other speculative investments.

That's what you're **told!**

You were told wrong. And, the majority of you still did exactly that.

Why are you not given any other options within your 401 K plan or your company savings plan that still have **good growth potential but no risk to your principle?**

Virtually all retirement savings plans involve a high degree of risk. If you have non-qualified money, the types of investments that I just mentioned are all taxed as capital gains **not** as ordinary income and this is the tradeoff for risking your money.

This is very important because generally speaking, half of your savings will be qualified money and half will be non-qualified money.

The non-qualified portion gets a much lower tax rate but much higher risk.

I personally think the federal government and Wall Street are most definitely in bed with each other on this issue.

They know you're pigeonholed and forced to put your money in the most tax efficient place and that floods money into Wall Street in equities, mutual funds, ETFs etc.

This is not fair to the average investor especially when in 2001 and 2008 we saw 401 K's become 201 K's or even 101 K's!

Even the most high quality index funds and mutual funds cannot withstand a bear market that affects all sectors of the economy. The averages are not going to help you here.

You always have to buy low and sell high. If you sell low, you lose your money! This is just not a risk that I want to subject my clients who are 60 or older to.

There is a way to have good growth, tax advantages, and complete safety of your money in **Indexed Insurance Products**.

The actuaries and financial gurus who came up with this concept back in 1996 created one of the greatest savings products ever and I believe a product that can be a **savior** for retirees!

My motto remains, "Most of the growth, none of the risk!"

Here are the details on how these products work.

When you purchase an indexed insurance product, the insurance company puts your money into what they call their "general account assets." Within that general account, the insurance company bears any and all investment risk.

In exchange for that, you get a contractual guarantee from that insurance company. That contractual guarantee says this:

You will never lose a dime of your principal, plain and simple.

The insurance company then purchases stock options (and these companies are very good at purchasing options) in a major stock index. As I mentioned before; that index is the S&P 500.

Disclaimer: there are other "boutique" indexes available that an insurance company can purchase options on. I don't usually like to recommend them because the S&P has the longest and best track record of consistent performance

The stock options in the major stock index are purchased to put the **"interest risk"** on contract holders. Interest risk is much different than traditional risk.

Your risk is with how much interest you're going to earn, not on whether or not you could lose any or all of your money!

So what's the downside?

The worst case scenario is you could earn 0% interest in any given year and because the insurance company bears all of the investment risk you don't get all of the gain in the major stock index.

But believe me, you get most of it.

The **best** case scenario is a **double digit** annual credited interest rate to your contract!

Here is where I need to make the most **important** distinction between **traditional investing** and **indexed insurance contracts.**

It is the difference between "credited interest" and "capital appreciation."

Credited interest is exactly what it sounds like, it's your money, it's credited to your account, you now own it, it cannot be taken away from you and it compounds annually!

Capital appreciation is a paper gain. And it can most certainly also be a paper loss. You own nothing other than the investment itself (shares of stock, mutual funds). **You must buy low and sell high, everything that happens in between is a "fugazi".**

It's not real!

But let's say you do sell off your investment positions when they're down 30% from the price that you paid for them. You'll see it takes more than a 30% gain to get back to even.

If you do the math, you'll see it takes a 42% gain just to get back to even.

After 22 years working with retired clients I can tell you, this is the biggest **threat** that their money faces!

As I mentioned before, a lot of retirees and people who are getting ready to retire are between a rock and a hard place. You want growth opportunities **and** to pay that lower capital gains tax rate but you don't want the risk of the market.

Here's how index insurance contracts work in this regard.

Interest earned in these accounts is taxed at the ordinary income tax rate however you get the tremendous benefit of **tax deferral** while it's growing.

This is a **triple benefit**: interest on interest, interest on gains and interest on the money that you would have normally paid in taxes.

Huge tax benefit for your non-qualified money!

So I think when you weigh it out, if you can capture a good portion of the growth of a major stock index and take **none** of the risk, it's worth it to pay the ordinary income tax rate on money that is actually **yours.**

The biggest objection I get when presenting this idea to clients is "I want all of the market gains, not a portion".

To this I say: The cumulative average annual rate of return for the S&P 500 from 1993 to 2017 was **4.43%**. In an indexed insurance contract crediting just **55%** of the growth of the S&P 500 **with none of the down years (or 0% credit in the down years)** the cumulative average annual rate of return was **5.86% or 132% of the index average!**

When you eliminate risk and replace it with annually compounded interest, the years in which there **is** a nice rate of return (a real rate of return not a paper gain) become much more powerful!

You're earning real interest that compounds in an account that can never go backward and lose value. You get to keep your gains every year and not have to worry about what the value of your account will be when you **actually need the money.**

Your money **will** work for you with an indexed insurance contract.

Chapter 5 – Longevity Risk

For a lot of people, the fear of death is being replaced by the fear of outliving ones resources; this is the essence of longevity risk.

In the past this wasn't a really a problem. But, modern medicine, healthier diets and a safer environment have put a lot of retirees in a position where they have to ask themselves an **important** question:

"Will I have enough money to sustain a comfortable lifestyle throughout my retirement?"

When people come into my office they're much less concerned with death, transferring wealth to loved ones and end of life healthcare expenses than they are with how much risk is within their portfolio and what their retirement income will be.

This translates into exactly what their lifestyle will be like in retirement. And, that is very, very important to most people.

In the previous chapter we looked at risk and provided a solution that allows you to take all of the risk out of your retirement nest egg.

That problem can be easily solved.

But, retirement income is a little trickier because you can only **generate** as much income as your <u>savings</u> will allow. This is where leverage is extremely important.

Just as important is safety.

So, the two most important steps in the retirement planning process are #1, eliminating risk; and #2, creating retirement income.

One more comment on risk... some of you reading this may want to, **"play with your money."** This means, **timing the market, day trading, and generally watching your nest egg like a hawk.**

That's fine if you have the knowledge and experience to **ensure** a successful outcome. But, most people do not have that knowledge and experience.

Generally, I find that my philosophy of retirement planning (eliminating risk and creating income) matches up with the philosophy of most folks.

When it doesn't, there is nothing I can do for you other than tell you, "Good luck!"

So, what does traditional retirement planning have to say about creating retirement income?

The general rule **used to be:** Withdraw 2 to 3% of your total assets per year and that should be enough to sustain you throughout retirement. This is based on again, those pesky "averages!"

And as I said before; the averages aren't on your side with a time horizon of 5 to 20 years.

Now the rule is: Withdraw 4% to 5% of your total assets per year to live on.

The idea being that at the end of your life, and your spouse's life, there is something left over to pass on to your beneficiaries.

All of this is completely dependent on how much money you have **saved.** My JOB as insurance and safety based planner is to make the most of what you **have saved**; no matter what it is and to create some form of leverage.

Traditional retirement planning does not have solutions that **include** leverage. Their solution is: have a balanced portfolio, take some risk and over the long-run everything will work out.

You see, they want your assets with them for your entire life because no matter what happens **they** collect their fees.

How "noble" of them!

That's why they don't want to make a recommendation outside of the scope of this type of plan, because if they did... they lose their fees! Ultimately, they are not in the business to help you but to guarantee their own profits.

Insurance-based plans are the only way to create leverage.

I understand these types of plans do have their drawbacks; which I'm going to cover more in Chapter 6. But, if you have decided that you don't want to risk your retirement nest egg any longer; **what are some other options available to you that don't involve insurance?**

Bank account: You have no leverage here with no tax advantages and certainly no way to guarantee retirement income.

The main problem with a bank account is that the interest is so ridiculously low that your principal would disappear so fast it would make your head spin!

Why?

Because the banks are paying next to nothing of interest so you would not be keeping pace with inflation; you would be eating into your principal!

Tax free municipal bonds or corporate bonds: The issue with a bond heavy brokerage account is that most brokerage accounts are designed for accumulation and growth while you are in your working years, not for creating retirement income that you can never out-live.

You **do** get tax advantages with municipal bonds and they can provide retirement income. However, this income does not come with any sort of "guarantee."

Bond strategies can be cumbersome and confusing and no matter what, there's always a risk of default even with government bonds.

When you try to move from an accumulation-oriented to a distribution-oriented strategy, you must remember that dividends, bond interest or bond funds can create an income stream, but there is **no lifetime guarantee** with any of these options for income!

So, your income may be fantastic one year and the next year cut in half!

Peace of mind comes when you have guaranteed income for life.

Having said that, I want the income you create to be flexible and not irrevocable!

Lastly, there's real estate: You may be in a position where you own a property and can generate positive cash flow from that property which can create retirement income. This can be a lot of work and there's no guarantee of that income either.

And, there's also no guarantee of what rate you'll be able to charge for rent for the rest of your retirement.

I think you get the picture: Guarantees and leverage are the pathway to peace of mind when it comes to retirement income.

Just to reiterate what I have said so far: <u>Longevity risk is the risk of outliving your resources in retirement which could put you in a position to become dependent on the state or social security as your only source of income</u>.

Which is certainly something no one wants to experience!

Risk and income are the two major concerns that every retiree has and should be creating a plan **early and often** to make sure that neither of these could disrupt a retirement that has peace of mind.

Traditional retirement planning does not have a way to guarantee income and eliminate risk.

Bond strategies can work but they're not perfect by any means.

Leverage is the key to creating retirement income.

So, how do we create leverage?

Traditionally, **annuities** have been the way to go. They are a unique animal, as insurance products go, because the insurance protection feature really comes into play the longer you live and that's where you have leverage.

Some insurance planners have made really bad recommendations in this regard however.

If you buy a life-only annuity and you don't live for a long time, you could lose substantial amounts of your retirement nest egg. As a result I never recommend life-only annuities!

Why?

Because you have not accomplished taking risk out of your situation, the insurance company could end up being a big winner if you purchase a life only annuity and your beneficiaries are the losers.

A life annuity with a guaranteed period certain option is most definitely a better bet.

In this situation you're guaranteed to get **at least** the amount of money you put into it back (or if you pass away early your beneficiaries will get the remainder of the money you put into it)

I still don't think that these are the best solutions for most retirees and here's why: Even with a life with period certain annuity you don't have a whole lot of **flexibility.**

Once you turn on that income stream it cannot be stopped and those payments will never increase and never decrease. They remain STATIC.

There is just not a lot of leverage here but a pretty good **solution** for those looking for retirement income.

My solution is a **lifetime income benefit rider** that's attached to a deferred annuity not to an immediate annuity.

This rider gives you the benefit of guaranteed lifetime income no matter how long you live plus the ability to start and stop that income anytime you want.

Let me explain exactly how the lifetime income benefit rider works because I think these products have been mis-sold and misrepresented and I want to make this crystal clear for you here.

Let's say you have two different "buckets" of money within a deferred annuity with a lifetime income benefit rider.

One bucket is the **cash growth bucket or accumulation value** which I will label, the **"emergency fund"** should you ever need to take the money out and not use it to create retirement income.

Most of you reading this book carry insurance for your car and insurance on your houses, condominiums or apartments.

Why do you?

Because even if you don't have a mortgage on your home and it burns to the ground you know that the insurance company will replace and rebuild your burned down home.

In other words it will be made whole again.

Well, why wouldn't you want to put an insurance policy around the largest or second largest asset you own, which in this case is your **retirement nest egg**, or accumulation bucket that you've grown for the last 25, 30 or 40 years of your life.

The other bucket is called the, **"income account value."** This value can never be cashed out in a lump sum because this is the value that the insurance company uses to calculate your lifetime income.

This bucket will grow at a guaranteed annual compound interest rate of somewhere between 6-8%, depending on what the insurance company is currently offering.

Also, most insurance carriers add a **bonus** to this bucket right from the beginning so you will **compound interest at a higher rate** right from the start.

When you're ready to start taking income, the insurance company applies a percentage, based on your age when you start the income, to the income account value.

The resulting number will be your guaranteed annual income for the rest of your life no matter how long you live!

If you want to **stop that income** at any time you can take the lump sum of what remains in the accumulation value or cash bucket.

This is much more flexible than a traditional income annuity that **can't** be stopped and is set in stone.

Here's an example: You position $100,000 in a deferred annuity with a lifetime income benefit rider.

The insurance company gives you an immediate 8% bonus on that money. Now, you have $108,000 growing at 7 1/2% for 10 years.

Then, you decide if you want to take your lifetime income.

In 10 years, your income account value is worth $223,000. Your withdrawal rate percentage is 6% at the age you take that income.

So, you're guaranteed a lifetime income after 10 years which translates into $13,380 per year for the rest of your life.

If you start that income at age 65 and you live to 90 years-old, you have leveraged your initial $100,000 to $334,500 over the course of 25 years!

And remember, that is guaranteed leverage with NO risk whatsoever.

There is one more interesting piece to this.

The insurance company has what they call an "income doubler" for nursing home or chronic health impairment.

This means they will double that income amount ($13,380) for up to five years should you have a major health impairment or be confined in a nursing home.

Now you're looking at **serious leverage!**

And this is all **guaranteed** through the insurance contract.

These products take longevity risk completely out of the picture even if you live to be 120 years old!

That income will never stop no matter what.

I see females looking at this product more seriously than men because they live longer and have a higher concern with longevity risk.

And, if you make this move early enough in your retirement say at age 55; you give the income account value a longer period of time to grow which will create even more guaranteed lifetime income.

This is yet another way to make your money work for you by keeping the two major concerns of retirees right at the forefront: **Risk and income!**

Chapter 6- Lack of Liquidity

Definition: Liquidity means how quickly you can get your hands on your cash. Or, in simpler terms, liquidity is the ability to get your money whenever you need it.

I would like to **reiterate** our philosophy before I start talking about this subject.

I believe that financial planning for **retirees** is a different proposition than for **younger** folks and the process involves these steps:

1. **Eliminating risk from your portfolio**
2. **Growing your wealth without risk.**
3. **Creating a sustainable income plan and leveraging assets to create lifetime retirement income that can also provide enhanced benefits for unexpected health care costs.**
4. **Providing leverage of current assets for health-related expenses as you are getting older.**
5. **Transferring wealth to beneficiaries on a tax-free basis.**

By now, you have seen that my philosophy **heavily involves** insurance contracts and insurance-based strategies. I talked a little bit about why some annuities have given the term, "annuities" a bad reputation.

The annuities that have created that stigma are detailed here:

A single premium immediate annuity with a <u>life-only</u> strategy is a bad investment because if you don't live a long time you may not get all of your money back.

A variable annuity is one of the worst financial products available and continue to be sold by the **billions**. They're bad because they are a quadruple whammy of **costs and fees, market risk and surrender charges.**

They are just not a very good way to go.

High surrender charge; long-term annuity plans. For people over the age of 60 investing in any financial product longer than 10 years is probably a bad idea, especially if the surrender charge percentage is 15% to 20% or more in the beginning years.

Two-tiered annuities. Two tiered annuities force you to defer the money for a **long** time and then force you to take income for an even **longer** time. It's a completely inflexible and terrible program.

There is no liquidity here and these products have spurred class action lawsuits against insurance companies and the sales agents. Thankfully, most two-tierd annuity products are no longer available for sale.

The only "good" that ever came from these products was big commissions for the sales agents and big profits for the insurance companies.

There's nothing good in any of these annuities for the average pre and post-retiree consumer.

Any good annuity contract should include the following 2 liquidity features:

1. A 10% or more free-withdrawal provision.
2. A waiver of all surrender charges should you go into a nursing home, need chronic health care or become terminally ill.

These features are **mandatory** for my annuity clients!

Now I want you to look at the **two** main insurance-based strategies that I've proposed thus far in a **different** light.

I believe, people over the age of 60 should be primarily concerned with **two** areas when it comes to their money; **the safety of their financial principal and the ease of access to it.**

If those two things are not in play, all the other ancillary benefits and strategies don't really mean anything at all.

If your money isn't safe and you can't get at it easily then what good is that PLAN?

Traditional retirement planning would tell you to have a **diversified** portfolio and ride out the ups and downs of the market and at the end of it all, you should have a nice rate of return and access to your money.

But, there is a major BUG in that ointment!

Is a traditional brokerage account or managed money portfolio really **liquid?**

Here is a clue...

It is **not.**

Let me explain **why.**

If you have a traditional Wall Street retirement portfolio and you need access to the monies within that portfolio at a time when the underlying securities have lost value (think 2001 or 2008) and you go to your advisor or broker and tell them you need money right **now** for your own reasons...

Guess what?

Your broker or advisor is going to do <u>everything</u> in his or her power to stop you from doing that!

Why?

Because if you pull funds out of those positions when your accounts are **down**, you have now realized a loss; a <u>real</u> loss, not just a **paper** loss.

Yes, brokerage accounts are popular and have traditionally been the standard advice that is given to everybody.

And why is that?

Because they are **liquid;** you can get at this money any time that you want!

No probelmo.

But making a withdrawal (selling securities) and starting an income strategy from your portfolio when your positions are **down** is a MAJOR problemo!

Because the truth is that in a traditional type retirement savings position you are not as liquid as you think.

I've already mentioned at the beginning of this chapter the **four** types of annuity contracts you should never purchase because they **do not provide adequate liquidity for most retirees!**

Let's contrast an insurance based strategy with the **safe position**- a bank CD, money market, or even a bond strategy.

Yes, you do have ample liquidity there but you do not have any of these things:

- **Leverage**
- **Lifetime income guarantees**
- **Opportunity for good growth**
- **And, absolutely no tax benefits**

Or, to humor it, "Other than that Goliath what is your overall impression of slingshots?"

Walk away from traditional investments and start looking at insurance-based strategies in a **new** and **refreshing** light.

I'm going to recommend a solution for those of you who really like the features that these products provide but don't want to tie your money up.

I want to restate the benefits that insurance-based solutions provide so you can fully understand why these are the strategies I recommend to my clients.

With these strategies you will receive all of the following:

Participation in market gains without any risk to principal

Growth that is credited as annual, compound interest (It's a real interest rate between 0-12%+ and not just a paper gain!) This growth **can never be taken away from you** due to a market correction.

A lifetime income stream that, dollar for dollar, can produce much greater amounts of income with the same pool of assets.

Income that is **flexible** and can be started or stopped and if you wish; you may withdraw a lump sum at any time. This is an income stream where the payment amount can be doubled should you need nursing home or chronic care.

Health Care protection that Medicare and traditional Health Insurance do not provide.

Leverage of your current assets to pay for care without buying expensive insurance. And, if no care is needed; you pay **nothing.**

Tax free wealth transfer with life insurance that is specifically designed for those 55 and older that is simpler to buy and to qualify for medically.

That is **WHY** I recommend these products to all of our clients!

I don't even believe it's **debatable** that these are very strong features.

What **is** debatable is this:

Do these insurance-based strategies provide enough **liquidity?**

In some cases, no, they don't.

Insurance-based strategies do come with a tradeoff; there may be a penalty if you withdraw all of your funds before the contract term expires.

But now I'm going to give you a solution to that problem.

It's those same insurance-based strategies but with the added benefit of what is called a **Return Of Premium rider (ROP).**

Simply put, this means that if the account is ever cashed out, you'll receive the greater of the current cash out value or the initial premium (principal) whichever is more.

Some of the single premium simplified issue index life insurance policies that I offer have this ROP rider.

Very few annuities have the ROP rider.

Why?

Because it can be a big loser for the insurance company and the insurance agent offering the product and money talks with these people.

When a product **isn't profitable** for the insurance company that usually means it's **very good** for the **consumer.** Again, if you like the benefits that I just outlined but you don't like the fact that your money may be tied up; this is the **solution!**

In many cases (and in my personal experience with actual clients) I have seen total cash out values that are **higher** than the initial principal amount after just one year with both the ROP annuity or simplified issue life insurance policies!

If there's an emergency or you simply want to put your money somewhere else; you have the ability to do that at **any** time with no early withdrawal penalty.

This is the way to go.

Most annuities and especially life insurance policies **do not provide this kind of liquidity**. This can give you tremendous peace of mind when making a switch to an insurance-based and speculation-free retirement strategy.

These products are hard to find because the insurance company will intentionally design other features of the product to be much less beneficial because the product has the return of premium rider which does not make the insurance company happy.

You need to speak with someone who knows about these kinds of products and the intricacies they contain.

There's only of a handful of them that I recommend to clients.

Put your money to work for you without sacrificing liquidity!

Chapter 7- Taxable Retirement Income

I explained in a previous chapter the reasons why I think the federal government and Wall Street are in cahoots, but I think it's critical here to **restate** my theory as it applies to the ways in which your retirement is taxed.

Yes, it is that important!

The ordinary income tax rate and the capital gains tax rate are very **different** and I think it's completely **unfair**, especially for retirees, to have to pay **more** in taxes on their wages and safe retirement money than they pay in taxes on their speculative investments.

This is the way that Wall Street insures that you have **speculative** investments rather than things to produce ordinary income.

Why?

Because potentially you could end up paying a lot less in taxes using the capital gains tax rate rather than the ordinary income tax rate!

The disparity between the two could be as much as 15%.

Does it make sense for you to risk your hard-earned money to pay lower taxes?

Most reasonable people would say no; but they do it anyway!

In the spirit of staying consistent with what I've done so far, let's **contrast** what traditional retirement planning, Wall Street and the banks have to offer you when it comes to **tax savings.**

Again, Wall Street incentivizes risk-taking by utilizing the current tax law which states, **"You pay less tax on your investments than you do on other interest bearing type accounts."**

That's crazy.

It's never made sense to me and never will but it is the way it is and it may not ever change.

Someone is making a lot of unethical money off you.

So, the case could be made, that keeping your money in speculative investments is a better position from a tax standpoint.

And, even though this may not be something that is ever explained to you by your advisor, I believe this is one of the reasons why the "professionals" advise you to put your money in stocks, bonds, and other types of speculative investments!

When it comes to the banks, I can't see any very solid solutions that they may be able to offer people with regard to taxation on their savings accounts.

Usually, what your banker would tell you is that they are not a tax attorney and can't give any tax advice. But, that is not the real reason.

The honest answer is that there is no advice to give here!

Bank accounts simply do not allow for your savings to grow in a tax favorable way. There's really only **one** less speculative type of investment that you might make that provides good tax benefits.

Tax free municipal bonds.

But they do have some **downsides.**

--They have low interest rates.
--They can sometimes be confusing and difficult to purchase.
--And even with government institutions, there's always a risk of default.

But generally speaking, I think tax free municipal bonds are a pretty good place for retirees to sock away money.

If we look at this as a whole, what is traditional retirement planning actually **doing** to minimize the taxation on your nest egg?

There are strategies that can be employed but almost all of them involve a degree of risk to **your** principal.

As you can guess, I'm not a big fan of that!

What is ideal is that retirement assets and retirement income should have the **least** amount of taxes due on them as possible from the beginning of retirement all the way to the end.

And, with very little or no taxes being paid by your beneficiaries.

If you agree that you want to pay as few taxes as possible on your money and your income in retirement, **this is for you.**

Now I'm going to present a solution that I wasn't a big fan of initially because of the complexities involved and honestly I just wasn't very knowledgeable about it and I asked myself,

"How in the world is this possible?"

In my mind, it just seemed too good to be true.

Years later and now with a lot more experience now; I understand exactly how it works. It is complex but if done the right way it can save you boatloads of money in taxes.

The name of the solution is **indexed universal life.**

I spoke about a certain type of life insurance in a previous chapter that was specifically designed for retirees; with simple underwriting and a one-time premium payment.

This is NOT that type of insurance.

Indexed universal life comes with full underwriting and multiple premiums.

So, if you have very poor health this will not be a strategy that you should employ. But, if you have decent health and you're in your or 60's or early 70's, this can be a terrific strategy.

So how does it work?

Let's begin with qualified accounts like IRA's, or a (401k). These accounts **seem** like a great way to save for retirement, you pay no taxes on any of the money that goes into these while you're working.

But, beware here.

Uncle Sam is your partner in retirement and somewhere between 10% and 30% of your IRA is his. It's not <u>ALL</u> your money!

These qualified accounts will **eventually** become completely taxable!

You will end up paying tax on the harvest and not the seed. The Federal government loves qualified accounts because they know eventually they're going to get their money.

Some experts recommend what's called, **de-qualification** of these accounts.

Here is where **indexed universal life** comes into play.

Let's say you're 60 years-old and have $150,000 in your IRA account. You would **de-qualify**, meaning pay the taxes, on $50,000 each year for three years, paying off all the tax on your $150,000 qualified account.

Those would be the three premium payments made into the indexed universal life policy. These would be after-tax payments. After three years you've now completely funded a retirement income account that will never be taxed again!

VOILA!

How does that work?

Specific tax codes that apply only to life insurance are used here. These codes allow you to take money out of your life insurance policy **tax free**.

The money you take out is characterized as a "loan" but as long as there is a decent amount of growth within the policy, **that loan will never have to be repaid.**

That's where **indexing** takes over.

Indexing allows these policies to grow at a better rate than a **fixed** interest type insurance policy. And that is growth without **any** risk.

The policy keeps growing along with the index and you keep taking loans as long as you need income in retirement and those loans are always tax free!

For non-qualified money the process works the same, but without the sting of paying the tax first.

Remember, you can never put qualified money into a life insurance policy. This is why I always ask my clients, **"Do you want to pay tax on the seed or the harvest?**

If you'd rather pay tax on the seed, this may be a good strategy. Indexed universal life is after all, <u>**life insurance**</u>.

These monies have to be inside a life insurance policy to take advantage of the tax codes.

So, with these policies not only can you access the cash values on a tax-free basis, there will always be a death benefit available to your beneficiaries upon your passing.

However, these policies must always be funded slowly (over 3-5 years) in order to not exceed the amount of cash value (allowed by the tax codes) in the policy for a given death benefit, which would negate the tax advantage.

Sound complicated?

It is. Don't try this on your own.

Chapter 8 – Insurance Companies and Agents

I've now presented you with what I believe are the seven greatest threats to your secure retirement.

I've also provided ample evidence that Wall Street, the banks and traditional retirement planning **cannot overcome** these threats in the same way that insurance-based and safety-based solutions can.

Some of you may be thinking, **"These solutions sound great and I want to implement them immediately!"**

But, some of you may also have good reasons in your mind why you wouldn't choose an insurance-based plan over a traditional type retirement plan or solution.

That's with good reason.

Most people simply do not see insurance companies as a place that can provide **financial solutions** for your retirement. They see insurance companies as **strictly providing** insurance solutions like traditional term life insurance, health insurance and property and casualty insurance.

If you want the safety, growth, income, guarantees and leverage that insurance-based solutions provide, you'll need to look at this in a **different** way.

It's my job to show you why insurance companies are some of the <u>best</u> partners for you all the way through your retirement. Not just for insurance but for protection and growth of your retirement nest egg.

I'm going to explain why insurance companies are a great partner for you and to do this I need to explain something very **important.**

In 2015, the Department of Labor put forth a new piece of legislation/regulation.

In addition to requiring more disclosure, best practices and establishing a fiduciary standard for fee-based advisors, it also proposed to apply those same standards to **insurance agents.**

This regulation would require that insurance agents selling products that have contractual guarantees of principal **were held to the same standard** as fee-based advisers selling risk and speculation.

This did not make any sense to me and and this is where the **role** of the insurance company - when it comes to your money - is very **important.**

Now this is just my opinion here but I think the **"fiduciary standard"** should only be placed on advisors who are offering investments that have **risk.**

If another 2001 or 2008 market correction were to happen, the value of your securities **could most certainly decline**.

The advisor recommending those securities to you has a responsibility to let you know how **much** risk you're taking and that **you could literally lose all of your money!**

That advisor bears that responsibility.

When I first saw this regulation put out by the Department of Labor I thought, "There's something fundamentally wrong with this!"

Insurance agents offering guaranteed insurance contracts that will never lose principal should not be held to the same standard as advisors offering securities where all of the principle could be lost!

The insurance company bears all of the investment risk. Not the insurance agent or the contract holder. This is so important to understand!

This is why I have so much passion for these products.

I can recommend something to you that has a **guarantee**, an **IRONCLAD** guarantee in fact, from a reputable, highly regulated insurance company with lots of assets.

Good news here.

That particular piece of legislation/regulation was thrown out by the Fifth Circuit Court of Appeals in 2018.

I believe cooler heads prevailed and they saw how absolutely **unfair** it was to place standards on insurance agents that shouldn't be there.

This does not mean that full disclosure and best practices should not be used.

When I work with clients I am so thorough, that by the time they make a decision to place money with an insurance company, there's absolutely no doubt in their mind as to what they're purchasing, how it works and ALL of its benefits and drawbacks.

The biggest take away here is that with all of the solutions that I've offered in this book, the insurance company bears **all** of the investment risk!

I've shown you how Wall Street, the banks and traditional retirement planning have many flaws but the biggest one is that most of the methods and advice they give is the same advice given to people of **any** age!

Big mistake.

Retirees have a much different situation than people who are <u>working</u> and this is always at the forefront of any planning I do.

When clients come to my office I show them this graphic of Mount Everest.

In the age of modern technology that we're in, **getting up the mountain** in retirement is getting easier.

Ebrokerages are emerging, and a lot of them employ different types of artificial intelligence to make investment recommendations. It's a cookie cutter approach based on basic data that investors provide to them.

As a retirement coach, my job is to help you get **down** the mountain.

I want you to not only survive your retirement but also to **thrive** in it! All of the solutions I've given you in this book involve insurance-based retirement plans.

Insurance companies are required to operate in a completely different way than Wall Street and the banks and this benefits YOU tremendously!

Insurance carriers are rated by **three** or more different ratings companies. And, to an insurance company, having a **bad financial strength rating** won't allow them to do the same volume of business as companies with **better** financial strength ratings.

In fact, I won't represent any insurance carrier with **less than a B+ rating by AM Best.**

In addition, the reserve requirements that insurance companies are subject to are the reason you get such an ironclad guarantee when you place your money with an insurance company.

Insurance companies must have at least $1 in reserve for every $1 on deposit! Banks do not have this requirement. There are **no reserve requirements** when you purchase securities.

There, you bear all of the investment risk!

If you like some of the alternative, insurance-based retirement strategies that I have recommended, you'll want to consult with an insurance agent or an advisor who **specializes in insurance**; specifically, annuities and life insurance.

It's important to mention exactly how insurance agents get paid when you buy an annuity or a life insurance policy. They are compensated with a **<u>commission NOT a fee.</u>**

There's a very important distinction here.

A **fee** is typically what you would pay on a managed money-type of account. This fee is charged to you no matter **how well or how poorly** your adviser does. And typically, it's charged annually by the firm that is managing your money.

This fee comes out of **your** money!

A **commission** is paid to an insurance agent by the insurance company that he or she does business with. Their commission is based on the amount of assets that you position with the insurance company.

This commission **does not** come out of **your** money ever!

Conclusion

In addition to the issues I've already covered, its important for retirees to also consider end of life planning. **ALL** retirees should have a comprehensive plan that may include a living will, medical directive, revocable or irrevocable trust for estate planning needs and a final expense trust for end of life planning. As well as proper Medicare and Social Security strategies.

It has been a great pleasure writing this book and I sincerely hope you not only learn from it but that you financially benefit from it as well!

Please give me a call if you have any questions on any of the material that you've read. I am more than willing to help you put these strategies into play!

All the Best,

Lance Ortiz

Made in USA - Crawfordsville, IN
64189_9781796836608
03.07.2023 1828